TAKING CARE

Mia McCullough

BROADWAY PLAY PUBLISHING INC
224 E 62nd St, NY, NY 10065
www.broadwayplaypub.com
info@broadwayplaypub.com

TAKING CARE
© Copyright 2008 by Mia McCullough

First printing: April 2007
I S B N: 0-88145-374-9

Book design: Marie Donovan
Word processing: Microsoft Word
Typographic controls: Ventura Publisher
Typeface: Palatino
Printed and bound in the U S A

TAKING CARE was developed in part through
the Womens Theater Alliance New Play Workshop,
and Chicago Dramatists.

TAKING CARE was originally produced by
Steppenwolf Theater Company (Martha Lavey,
Artistic Director; Michael Gennaro, Executive Director),
opening on 6 March 2003. The cast and creative
contributors were:

MA ....Rosalyn Alexander
BENNY ....Guy Van Swearingen

Director...............................Tim Hopper
Scenic design ....Russell Poole
Costume design ....Jennifer Roberts
Lighting design ....Adam Friedland
Sound design ....Joshua Horvath
Stage manager ....Malcolm Ewen
Dramaturg ....Edward Sobel

CHARACTERS & SETTING

BENNY, *a man in his forties*
MA, BENNY's *mother, seventy-six at start of play.*

Various voices heard on the television or radio.
All prerecorded.

Time: 1996 to 2003

Place: A small apartment that has not altered in appearance in many years.

AUTHOR'S NOTE

BENNY is an unmedicated schizophrenic. I no longer refer to his specific illness in the play because audiences have gotten very caught up in their own misconceptions of what schizophrenia is, and I have no interest in turning my play into a psychology lesson. For the audience members, I don't think the diagnosis is relevant as long as BENNY's behavior is clearly that of someone who is not well.

For the actor playing BENNY, the diagnosis is important. BENNY has been ill since his teen years. He has never been medicated and he no longer exhibits many positive symptoms (positive symptoms include hallucinations, lashing out in a violent manner, speaking non-sensically). For the most part, he exhibits negative symptoms of which the most obvious is withdrawing from human contact and communication. Schizophrenics are prone to compulsive and repetitive behaviors, and those behaviors tend to become more exaggerated when they are agitated. Often, as schizophrenics pass into their forties and fifties, the disease releases some of its hold on them.

TAKING CARE is inspired by actual events.

Scene 1

(*A small and slightly dingy apartment. The furniture is tacky. Ornately carved wood, stained white with faded upholstery that was once loud and garish. Shawls and throws cover everything. Downstage two armchairs and a small coffee table face a large, old . Stage left is a daybed. Upstage is the kitchen area. A refrigerator and a sink are along the back wall. A table, about twice the length of a card table divides the kitchen area from the living room. There are three chairs around this table, and a small portable T V is set on top of it. A hallway leads to the bedroom and bathroom. The door to the apartment is stage left. On the wall is a portrait of a woman in her thirties, a portrait of a man in his thirties, and between them their wedding photo. The wedding photo hangs askew on its hook.*)

(BENNY, *a man in his forties, sits at the kitchen table watching T V. He has long hair, but it's matted and gnarled into a mass.* MA, *a woman in her seventies enters from the hallway carrying two full grocery bags. She is addressing someone in the hall.*)

MA: Yes, Mrs Heinemann. Yes. Yes, I'll have a talk with him..... Of course...I understand. I'll see you later. (*She closes the door with her behind.*) Uh! You're going to have to cut your hair. You're scaring the neighbors. (*She sets the groceries on the table. She takes out a prescription bottle and squints at the label.*)

MA: Here. These are yours.

(MA *sets the bottle down in front of* BENNY. *She begins pulling out own prescription medication.* BENNY *takes his bottle and tosses it in the trash.*)

MA: Don't do that! Don't throw them out. Those pills
cost a lot of money. Don't take them if you don't want
to, but don't insult me by throwing them out! *(She pulls
the pills out of the trash and sets them on the counter.)*
I don't know what the hell is wrong with you. Two pills
a day. Believe me, two pills is not such a chore. How
many pills do I take a day? Eight, sometimes twelve.
You don't see me complain.

BENNY: You complain.

MA: Shut up. The point is, I do it. I take the pills
because I'm supposed to. I don't waste them.

BENNY: I told you not to buy them.

MA: That would be...that would be... What do they call
it? Aiding and abetting. That's not right.
Co-dependent. No. What's the word I'm thinking of?

*(BENNY ignores MA, watching T V. She puts groceries
away.)*

MA: You could be well. You could be just as normal as
anyone, as me, if you'd take two pills a day.

BENNY: I never felt normal.

MA: You didn't give it a chance.

BENNY: You don't know.

*(While MA talks, she makes two identical sandwiches. As she
works she takes a dish rag from a hook by the sink and flings
it over her shoulder.)*

MA: I never should have been so easy on you....
You were always so difficult and I let it slide.
Your sisters are right about that. I treated you better.
Obviously, a huge mistake. But I will not give in to your
unwillingness to help yourself. I won't do it. Fine if you
won't take your pills. You can let them sit on a shelf
and stare back at you. Remind you that it's no one's
fault but your own that you're like this. You know

some things they don't have a cure for. Some things they can't fix at all. You at least, you they have medication for, and what do you do? Waste it. Here's your sandwich.

(MA *sets a sandwich in front of him.* BENNY *picks it up and begins to eat without acknowledging her. She takes her own sandwich and sits down in her armchair. He gets up, grabs the dish towel off her shoulder and carefully puts it back on the hook, then returns to his sandwich. She shakes her head. Pause)*

MA: Ethelyn Goodman died last night. Stroke. Only seventy-three. You remember her? The one with the bubble voice?

(No response, though BENNY *does glance over at* MA.*)*

MA: She's my only friend who wasn't afraid of you.

(Lights fade to bluck as they eat in silence. The T Vs flicker in the darkness and white noise swells. Different voices of T V personalities overlap one another.)

WEATHERMAN: *It's a blustery one out there today. Looks like autumn is really here. Tonight's temperature will be in the low...*

NEWS WOMAN'S VOICE: ...reporting on last night's Academy Awards ceremony....

Scene 2

(MA sits in her armchair on the phone. The cradle is on the wall behind her, and the cord is long enough to reach anywhere in the playing area.)

MA: Oh, you know. Nothing changes. I'm surviving. How's Kayla doing? ...She must be getting big. I wish you'd visit more often.... How is that husband of yours? ...I know he has a name.... I wasn't insulting him.

Believe me, if I wanted to insult him, I'd do it right....
Oh, you know. He's the same. No, he's out right now.
Smoking, loitering, I don't know. Oh, wait, his coat
is here. He can't be out. He must be sitting in the
bathroom... How should I know what he does? He has
that chair in there. Sits for hours.... So then I tell him to
get out, and he gets out.... Yeah. You know, he cut his
hair.... No he didn't let someone, he cut his own hair.
Well, how do you think it looks? The boy's never been
to beauty school.... It's a sight. I can't say it looks better.
Nearly gave me a heart attack to see it all lying there in
the garbage can when I got up in the morning. It looked
like his whole head was in there. *(She laughs.)* You talk
to your sister? She called last week. Sounds like she's
doing well at that job.... Yeah... Busy. Everybody's busy.
Everybody but me.

*(BENNY enters from the back. His hair is shorter, but not
neater.)*

MA: Oh, here's your brother. Coming out of his lair.

*(BENNY makes his way over to the kitchen table, ducking
under the telephone cord that is stretched across his path.)*

MA: *(Into phone)* I don't know why you always do this.

(To BENNY) Benny. Benny, you want to talk to your
sister?

BENNY: No.

MA: You hear that? Benny, talk to your sister. She wants
to talk to you. He's coming. It's Sharon.

(BENNY walks over to MA and takes the receiver.)

BENNY: Hi. *(Pause)* Okay.

*(Pause. While BENNY talks, MA gets up and straighten the
wedding photo on the wall. BENNY straightens the throw
that hangs on the back of MA's chair.)*

BENNY: Yeah. *(Pause)* Yeah. Okay.

(BENNY *hands the phone back to* MA, *tilts the wedding photo back to the way it was, and then goes and sits at the table in the kitchen and turns on the T V.)*

MA: I don't know why you bother. It's like talking to a potato. I may as well live by myself for all the company he is. Of course he's not taking the medicine.... You want to come over and shove the pills down his throat, be my guest.

(BENNY *turns up the volume.)*

MA: Not so loud!

(BENNY *turns it down, but gives* MA *a resentful glare.)*

MA: You and Shayna had better decide what it is you're doing with him when I die. The neighbors won't stand for him here and he can't take care of himself. I do everything for him. I cook, I clean. "You know, you know." Stop saying you know. You'll know when I die and he has to move into your house.... So, what? He's going to live with Shayna? ...Well, have you even discussed it? ...You're right, I'll be dead and it'll be none of my business. Did you ever think it might give me some peace to know what will happen to him? ...How can you say that, Sharon? If I didn't care he'd be out on the street.... No, he's not listening, he's watching T V. He never pays attention to a word I say, he never did. None of you ever did.... Why do I start? Does it ever occur to you that maybe you start? ...Oh, that's right, I forgot. I am the horrible woman and you are the innocent children.... Yes, that's fine. Goodbye. *(She gets up to hang up the phone.)*What did I do to deserve such miserable children? The whole lot of you. Your sisters say it's my fault they never visit. They make up these wild stories. These horrible things I've done to them. If I'd done such things, don't you think I would remember? I swear, they're crazy. How could I have

driven them away? What could I have done? I didn't
drive you away. You're still here.

(BENNY *gives* MA *a quizzical look.*)

MA: You, who I would like a break from now and
again. You have never left the nest.

BENNY: I left.

MA: You came back.

(MA *goes over and inspects the back of* BENNY's *head.
He waves her hand away as if swatting at flies.*

MA: I could even it up a bit.

BENNY: No!

MA: Fine.

(MA *pours two glasses of juice and puts five crackers each on
two plates, during this she puts the dish rag on her shoulder
again. She sets one glass and one plate in front of* BENNY,
*then takes her own snack over to her chair. She pulls out a
little portable table for her food and sets it on top.* BENNY
*pulls the schmata [dish rag] off her shoulder and puts it back
on its hook.*)

(MA *turns on her own T V and looks for something to watch.*
BENNY *sits back down and takes a bite of a cracker.*)

MA: I'll bet they put you in a home.

(BENNY *looks at* MA. *He stops chewing.*)

MA: Maybe they'll put us both in a home.

(*Lights fade. the T Vs flicker in the darkness. In the half light,*
MA *clears away her dishes and* BENNY's. *He gets up puts his
coat on and exits. She settles down into her chair and falls
asleep.*)

Scene 3

(MA *is asleep in her armchair. The door to the hall opens*
and BENNY *enters. He sees her asleep in the chair, and he*
purposefully closes the door loudly enough to wake her up.
She stirs and turns around to see him hanging up his jacket.
He is obsessive about how the jacket hangs from the hook.
He futzes with it until it's just right.)

MA: How can you wear that coat in this heat? I've never
understood that about you.

(BENNY *crosses the room and sits on the daybed. He stares at*
MA, *waiting.*)

MA: I suppose you want me to go to bed.

(*They look at one another.*)

MA: You'd think I'd be past waiting up for you by now.
I'm always afraid you won't come back.... I've never
gotten over you running off to California like that.
My baby, my boy, picking up and leaving. Driving to
the other side of the world with a bunch of who-knows-
what and you didn't even say goodbye. I know it
wasn't always the happiest home, I know, but I think
I deserved a goodbye, at least. I don't think I can ever
forgive you. For making me afraid like that. Like this.

(BENNY *shrugs and looks away.*)

MA: Well goodnight, then.

(MA *gets up with effort. She's stiff. The schmata is draped*
over her shoulder. She waddles off towards the back. As she
passes, BENNY *grabs at the schmata but she beats him to it,*
yanking it off her shoulder and then throwing it at him. He
hangs it in its spot as she exits. He straightens the throw on
her chair. He reaches under the daybed and takes out a pillow
and some blankets. He arranges them on the daybed. He

*grabs the remote and turns on the T V with the volume very
low. He curls up on the daybed, with the covers over him.)*

*(The lights fade. the T Vs flicker in the darkness. In the
half-light,* BENNY *gets up and puts away his bedding.*
MA *enters and pulls out a menorah from a cabinet which
she sets it on the table. He moves the menorah to a slightly
different position and sits at the table.)*

Scene 4

*(*BENNY *is watching his T V.* MA *sets a box of Hanukkah
candles on the table.)*

MA: You want to pick out the candles?

*(*BENNY *turns off the T V. He pulls out two candles, putting
one in the Shamas spot and one in the right-most spot. He
pulls out another candle and switches it with the Shamas.*
MA *is rifling through the kitchen drawers.)*

MA: I know I have matches around here somewhere.

*(*BENNY *takes out a lighter and flicks it on.)*

MA: You can't use that. You don't celebrate ancient
miracles with Bic lighters.... Here we go. Would you
like to light the Shamas or should I?

*(*BENNY *takes the matches and lights the Shamas.* MA *then
lights the first candle with the Shamas and sets it back in the
menorah.)*

MA: Well. Happy Hanukkah. Here's your Hanukkah
gelt.

*(*MA *holds out a dollar.* BENNY *shakes his head, amused.)*

MA: You don't want it?

*(*BENNY *takes the money before she can put it back in her
purse.)*

MA: That's what I thought. Your sisters yell at me for treating you like a child, but lord knows you don't discourage it. (*She puts her coat on.*)

MA: Somedays I wonder, when I die, will you turn into a man? Will you function? Or will you need someone else to be your mother?

(*They look at one another a moment.*)

MA: Well, I'm off to the party, then. Your supper's on a plate in the ice-box.... You sure you don't want to come?

(BENNY *shakes his head.*)

MA: Your Aunt Beena said it would be all right if you just sat in the den and watched T V. She wants the whole family to be together.

(BENNY *shakes his head again.*)

BENNY: Ma, could you turn the light down?

(MA *dims the light.*)

MA: All right. Don't go for your walk until the candles are all out.

(MA *exits.* BENNY *watches the flames as the lights fade. The T Vs flicker in the darkness. He slowly blows out each of the candles. He very carefully brings the menorah and the candles into the kitchen area and puts them away out of sight.*)

Scene 5

(BENNY *is watching the big T V. He is pacing back and forth, agitated, smacking himself in the head.*)

BENNY: No! Stupid, stupid, STUPID! What is electromagnetic! Magnetic! ...Duke of Wellington, what is the Duke of Wellington...I don't know. No... Oh! Oh! The Magna Carta! WHAT IS THE MAGNA CARTA!

God, you people are idiots! ...No, don't risk that much.
You're going to lose it. You don't know anything about
opera.

(BENNY *hears a key in the lock. He rushes up to the T V and
turns it off, then retreats to the kitchen.* MA *is talking to a
neighbor in the hallway.*)

MA: Yeah, it was a beautiful service. Very nice... Yes...
Not a good day to be standing outside wearing black,
but what can you do? *(She enters the apartment. She closes
the door on whoever it is.)* Yeah, okay. See you later.

(MA *shuts the door and lets out a weary sigh. She is in a
black dress and a black hat. She goes to her chair and sits
without looking at* BENNY *who is watching her. Pause)*

BENNY: Who died?

(MA *turns around and gives* BENNY *a hard stare, though she
is not in the least startled to find him there.)*

MA: Who died? *(Pause. She turns back and faces out.)*
Your father's cousin Ruth. You remember Cousin Ruth?

BENNY: Yeah.

MA: Well, she's dead.

BENNY: *(Unemotional)* You didn't tell me.

MA: I told you. I told you. You just weren't listening to
me. As usual.

BENNY: *(Matter-of-fact)* You didn't tell me.

MA: You must have heard me talking about it on the
phone.

BENNY: I don't listen to you on the phone.

MA: Ha.

BENNY: You didn't tell me.

MA: What? You were going to go to the funeral?

BENNY: No.

MA: So what does it matter if I didn't tell you? *(Pause)*
But I did. I remember telling you. *(A long pause. She
takes off her shoes and her hat. She is exhausted.)* Everyone
asked after you. "How's Benny?" "How's Benny
doing?" "Oh, you know, he's fine. The same. Nothing
changes." *(Beat)* What am I supposed to say? "Oh,
Benny? He's good. He met a nice girl and they got
married in a small, private ceremony, and now he's
got a successful textile business in Philadelphia and a
baby on the way." *(Pause)* Sometimes I make up a whole
life for you. I name your kids.... I even kind of like your
wife. But I never tell people about it when they ask.
About your make-believe life. I'm probably the only
one who would think it was funny. Get me a glass
of juice, will ya? There's always too much standing
around at these things.

*(BENNY gets up and pours a glass of juice and brings it over,
then goes back to his kitchen seat.)*

MA: Your cousin Alyssa said she saw you the other day.
She was driving down the street and she saw you
walking. She said she slowed down and called out to
you, but you looked at her and kept going. Didn't you
know it was her?

(Pause. BENNY stares at the little T V.)

BENNY: I knew.

MA: So, it would have killed you to stop and say hello?

BENNY: I don't like her.

MA: You used to play with her all the time when you
were kids.

BENNY: She used to play with me.

MA: She's a very nice woman now.

BENNY: She's stupid.

MA: She's not stupid. She's a doctor. Who are you to call other people stupid?

(*No response.* MA *gets up and carries her shoes and hat into the back.* BENNY *watches T V.*)

BENNY: (*Quietly*) What is osmosis.

MA: (*O S*) Did you say something?

BENNY: No.

(MA *returns without her jacket and with house slippers on her feet. She goes back to the chair. Big sigh*)

MA: So that's the last of your father's family. Well, you know, your cousins, but no one left to carry on the family name. You were the last one. The line dies with you.

BENNY: What do you care?

MA: I care...I care. Your father was so happy when he had a son. For a while.

(*Long pause*)

BENNY: So, what's my wife's name?

MA: Rachael.

(*Lights out. the T Vs flicker in the darkness.* MA *gets up and puts her glass in the sink. She puts the schmata on her shoulder and opens the fridge.*)

Scene 6

(BENNY *sits at his table.* MA *carries a piece of cake with a candle on it to him, cupping the flame with her hand, singing. She sets the cake in front of him.*)

MA: Happy Birthday Dear Benny, Happy Birthday to You. That's the kind you like, right?

(BENNY *nods. He leans forward to blow out the candle.*
MA *stops him with a fairly fierce yank of the shoulder.)*

MA: Make a wish first!

(BENNY *stares at* MA *long and hard. He grabs the rag off her
shoulder and puts it back on the hook, then returns to his seat
and blows out the candle. She hands him a long rectangular
package.)*

MA: Here.

(BENNY *unceremoniously unwraps the gift. It is a carton of
cigarettes.)*

BENNY: Thanks.

MA: Use them in good health. *(She laughs at her own joke
and sits down.)* At least you're easy to shop for, Benny.

(MA *turns on the T V. They both watch. After a moment:)*

BENNY: Did Sharon or Shayna call?

MA: Not yet. They might have forgot. We're not a high
priority with those two, you know. Not top of the list.
Uh! So dusty. Where does it all come from? The
windows are closed, we don't drag dirt up three flights
of stairs. It's never made any sense to me. *(She grabs a
rag and begins to wipe down surfaces and tchotckes.)*

BENNY: They always call.

MA: Yeah, well, some year they won't. Maybe this year.
You can't count on people, Benny, not even your sisters.
If there's one thing I've learned in life, it's that you can't
count on anyone.

(Pause. MA *continues to dust. She wipes across the radio and
accidentally turns it on. She tunes it and finds a station with
Lawrence Welk-ish music.)*

MA: I wonder if we just sat here in our chairs perfectly
still for months and months, if we died and your sisters
never came looking for us—which is not so out of the

realm of possibility—would the dust pile up like snow?
And how much? Would it ever stop?

BENNY: They call almost everyday.

MA: And you never want to talk to them. Why do you
care if they remember your birthday? I remembered.
Isn't that enough?

(MA *moves onto the photos on the wall. She straightens the*
wedding photo. She dusts her own photo first, then she takes
the photo of the man off the wall and dusts it ever so gently.
After a moment she begins to sway a little, then dance and
twirl with the photo held up like a partner. BENNY *looks on*
with irritation.)

MA: Your father was so handsome. It's too bad he hated
dancing. I would've liked to have gone dancing a time
or two. I guess we never had any money, anyway.
(She twirls around.) Well, you're dancing now, aren't
you, Saul? *(She stops, out of breath. She wipes the glass*
tenderly with her rag.)

BENNY: He left you. He moved out and then he died.

(MA*'s spell is broken.)*

MA: How would you know what happened? You
weren't here. You were in California getting high
and wandering the streets with no shoes on.

BENNY: Sharon and Shayna told me.

MA: Well, your sisters don't know everything. Your
father and I had a good marriage. Thirty-four years.

BENNY: He didn't even like you.

(Pause)

MA: Get out! Get out of my sight if you're going to say
such horrible things to me!

(BENNY *and* MA *stare each other down for a long moment.)*

MA: Get out!

(BENNY *turns off the T V, gets up, grabs his coat, puts it on carefully, buttoning every other button.*)

MA: He didn't like you either!

(BENNY *slams the door closed as he leaves.* MA *hangs the photo back on the wall. She goes over to the window, perhaps looking for him. Outside is the faint sound of an ice cream truck passing, children playing and shouting. As the lights fade a strong wind swells and buffets against the windows replacing the sounds of children. Dry leaves swirl in the wind. She backs away from the windows and slowly retreats to her bedroom as a snow plow goes by outside. A voice from a megaphone outside:*)

MEGAPHONE: If you are parked on the north side of the street, please move your vehicle immediately so we can plow. If you're parked on the north side.... (*The voice fades.*)

Scene 7

(MA *is at the wall by the phone wearing a bathrobe. She is frantically speaking into the receiver.*)

MA: Hello! Hello! Yes, my son is missing. Yes... I need someone to go out and look for him.... He lives with me. No, no, he always comes home. He goes out for his ten o'clock walk and then he comes home, watches television and goes to bed.... He's forty-five. No, you don't understand. He's not like a regular person. He's ill. No, not like he has the flu. He's mentally ill.... You don't understand, he does the same exact thing every day. Watches the same programs, eats the same things. Goes for walks.... Well, I don't know where he walks, exactly. I don't follow him. The point is, he should be home by now. He should've been home last night and

it's minus ten outside. He might be frozen to death on a
park bench.... No, I haven't looked for him. I'm eighty
years old. You want me to go outside, walk on the ice
and break my neck? Is that what you want? Maybe
if the city cleared the sidewalks, maybe then I could
go out and look for my son.... His name is Benjamin
Painter. Yes, with a "P". ...No, he's not retarded, he's
crazy.... No, not dangerous. He's a gentle boy, wouldn't
hurt a fly. I...I can't talk to you anymore. *(She hangs up
and immediately begins to make another call.)* Ignorant...
The machine... Sharon? Sharon? Are you there? ...This is
your mother.... Sharon, your brother didn't come home
last night, will you pick up the phone? ...I knew you
were there. Your brother never came home last night....
No, we didn't have a fight. We don't even speak, how
could we have a fight? ...I called the police, but you
have to call them back. I can't talk to those people... Yes,
I explained all that, they don't understand.... *I* should
call the hospitals? Why can't you call the hospitals?
...It's my fault you live long distance? I didn't tell you
to move half way across the country. I want to keep this
line open in case Benny calls...I don't know if he knows
the number. I don't know....

(The front door opens and BENNY *steps inside. He does not
close the door or take his coat off. He is shaking.* MA *drops
the phone as she runs to him.)*

MA: Benny! Oh, my God. Did you stay out in this all
night? Don't you have any sense? You've had me
worried sick! On the phone with the police! With your
sisters!

*(*BENNY *tries to take off his coat, but his fingers are too stiff.
He falls against the wall.)*

BENNY: There's something wrong with my feet.

MA: Your feet? What's wrong with your feet?

BENNY: I can't feel them.

(Lights fade to black. the T Vs flicker in the darkness. BENNY *exits.* MA *goes into the back.)*

(Ambulance sirens can be heard in the distance as the wind swells again. The siren grows closer and closer, then fades.)

*(*BENNY *enters from the back rooms with a walker and his feet bandaged. He walks gingerly. He grabs one of the chairs from the kitchen table and pushes it downstage with his walker. He sits in it and lights a cigarette.)*

Scene 8

*(*BENNY *sits in one of the kitchen chairs, smoking. He leans down a little to blow the smoke out an unseen window in the fourth wall. His feet are wrapped in bandages. Behind him, next to his chair is a walker.)*

*(*MA *enters from the back rooms.)*

MA: Jesus! It's freezing in here! Will you shut that window?

BENNY: I'm smoking.

MA: Well, stop it. Stop all of it. It's minus ten degrees out there! If it weren't for your smoking, you wouldn't have been outside in this and you wouldn't have lost three of your toes. *(She looks at the clock.)* I'd better change your bandages while I'm thinking of it. Put that out and close the window.

*(*MA *exits to the back rooms.* BENNY *sucks on the cigarette, getting the last puffs out of it. Then he puts it out in a tea cup. She returns with gauze, sterile tape and a tube of ointment. He shuts the window as she drags a tray table up and sets up her first aid materials.)*

MA: I guess the upside of this is you have to wash your feet every day. Maybe I can get the doctor to tell you to wash the rest of you everyday. Or every other day.

Even that would be a vast improvement. You know
your nieces won't even come to visit because it smells
so bad in here. That's why they don't come to see me.
Because you stink. I don't even notice anymore. *(She
pulls a chair up opposite of* BENNY *and sits.)* Okay, which
foot do you want to start with?

*(*BENNY *stares at* MA *meanly. He does not respond or move.)*

MA: You know, I could have let you be
institutionalized. That doctor asked me, "Does Benny
take his medication?" I say, "No, of course he doesn't.
He never takes his medication." And then the doctor
said, "Well, this incident seems indicative that Benny is
a danger to himself. It's enough to have him committed
to the psychiatric unit. And if he was committed they'd
make sure he took his medicine." And I said, "Oh, no.
Benny and I are fine. This was a one time thing. I don't
know why he didn't come home that night, but I'm sure
he's learned his lesson and it will never happen again,
Doctor." That's what I said to him. That's what I did
for you. Because if they put you in one of those places,
you'll have people telling you what to do every
moment of the day, and they'll put you on that
Thorazine stuff, and then you'll find a real appreciation
for your horrible mother. Your sisters thought
maybe we should, but I said no. Because they don't
understand what a nice arrangement we've got here.
So you've got to cooperate. Start behaving yourself.
You can't be doing these crazy things ever again,
Benny, or else we are both going to get put in a home.
Do you understand?

*(*MA *gives* BENNY *a moment to let this sink in.)*

MA: So what's it going to be? Which one of those
decapitated little piggies do you want to start with?

*(*BENNY *lifts one leg up, and after a second, lets it rest gently
on* MA's *knee.)*

MA: All right, then.

(MA *begins to unwrap the bandage as the lights fade. The T Vs flicker in the darkness. In the half-light she pulls off both bandages and takes them and her first-aid stuff into the back.* BENNY *folds up his walker and puts it in the closet. She brings out his shoes and he puts them on, methodically tying the laces. Outside, perhaps the sound of birds in spring.*)

Scene 9

(*Lights up on the apartment. There is a banging on the front door, a jiggling of the door knob, the sound of keys.* BENNY's *coat is on its peg, but he's nowhere in sight.*)

MA: (*Off stage*) Benny! Benny! Are you in there? Will you let me in? Benny! ...No, Mrs Heinemann, I'm fine. Something happened to the lock. My key isn't—oh, there it goes. No, I'm fine, thank you. Bye. (*She enters the apartment with her purse and a couple of grocery bags.*) Benny? Are you here? Of course, you're here. (*She gives his jacket a swat, knocking it from it's hook. Yelling*) What's wrong with you that you can't come to the door?

(MA *begins to put groceries away. The phone rings.*)

MA: Hello? Shayna? Why are you calling me now in the middle of the afternoon. What? ...I'm fine. He called you? ...I'm fine. I lost track of what floor I was on and tried to get into his apartment. It's not a crime, I was just distracted.... I was thinking and I didn't notice which floor I was on. I do think, you know.... Let me ask you something: Does everyone in this building have your number? Do they? What about that idiot across the hall? ...Look, I've got to put the lox in the fridge. I know it can reach, but I don't want to talk to you anymore, so goodbye. (*She hangs up the phone.*) Nosy good for nothin'. (*She stomps her floor on the floor, sending a message to her downstairs neighbor. She resumes putting the groceries away.)* That stupid goy who lives downstairs called your sister on me. It was an innocent mistake, and everyone's got to act like I'm losing my mind. All the floors look the same. Bastard got me so flustered I couldn't open my own door, followed me halfway up the stairs, everybody peeking out their doors at me. Who could open anything with such an audience of nosy-bodies? *(She shuffles over to the T V, hits the power and collapses into her chair.)* What's the matter with the T V? *(She gets up, turns it on and off a few times.)* What the...? *(She checks to see if it's plugged in.)* Is the power out? *(She turns a lamp on and it works.)* Benny, what did you do to my T V?! Benny, get out here...I said, get out here!

(BENNY comes out from the bathroom with a mixture of trepidation and defiance.)

MA: What did you do to my T V?

BENNY: Nothing.

MA: Don't lie to me, Benny. I know you watch it when I'm out. I hear you scurrying around in here when I'm outside the door. I'm not stupid, you know, now what did you do it?

BENNY: Nothing. It's not working. *(He sees his coat on the floor, and goes over to hang it up and fix it.)*

MA: I can see that it's not working. Did you hit it? Did you get excited watching your game show?

BENNY: It's not on until three.

MA: Was the television talking to you? Is that why you broke it?

BENNY: No. I didn't break it. It stopped working.

MA: So you were watching it.

BENNY: I didn't break it. *(He sits at his table.)*

MA: Well, what am I supposed to do? What am I supposed to do for company, now?

(BENNY *does not respond. Reflexively he looks at his T V, maybe even reaches to turn it on, but then realizes he'd rather not call attention to his T V.* MA *glowers at him.*)

(*Lights fade.* BENNY *turns on his T V. In the half light* MA *searches in some drawers and pulls out a deck of cards. She sits down next to* BENNY *and starts dealing for a game of solitaire. He scoots his chair a little further away from her.*)

Scene 10

(BENNY *sits at the kitchen table watching the mini T V.* MA *sits next to him playing solitaire. He watches her play out of the corner of his eye. When he can take it no longer, he reaches over and moves her cards.*)

MA: *I'm* playing.

BENNY: You suck.

MA: It doesn't matter. I don't want your help.

BENNY: You never win.

MA: (*Not talking about the cards*) No. I never do. Not in my whole life. (*Pause*) You watch stupid programs.

(MA *continues to play.* BENNY *watches the cards out of the corner of his eye.*)

BENNY: You're cheating.

MA: Shut up.

(MA *throws down the cards in frustration. Black out.*)

(*Lights come up again briefly on* MA *watching* BENNY'*s T V, which she has pulled over to her side of the kitchen table. She is laughing at the show along with the laugh track. He sits watching, not amused. Lights fade.*)

(In the half-light, BENNY *picks up each card, and squares up the deck as evenly a possible, checking it from every angle before he slides it into its box. He puts it back in the drawer in the kitchen.)*

Scene 11

(The lights come up on MA *in her chair, wrapped in blankets and an afghan.* BENNY's *T V is back in it's spot and a new T V sits on an ottoman. It's bigger than his but smaller than the original.)*

(The phone rings. MA *gets up to answer it.)*

MA: Hello? ...Lois! Where are you? Are you home? *(She crosses to downstage, peering out the "window" in the fourth wall and across the street. She waves energetically.)* Hi!... Happy Thanksgiving to you, too. Can you believe this? Two feet and it's only November... I know. We may not get out for a walk until April. *(She looks across the street at her friend and nods sadly. Then she makes her way to the stove and turns the heat on under a kettle, puts the schmata on her shoulder.)* I know. It makes you see why everyone moves to Florida.... Yes, you're right. Prisoners of Mother Nature.... I know. *(She shuffles back to her chair and sits.)* Oh, you know, it was good.... Yes, the girls are fine.... No, I didn't cook. I haven't cooked a big meal in I don't even remember. No, Sharon and Shayna cook? If they do, they keep it secret from me. All they ever want is to go out. Always in a restaurant where it's distracting and loud and you can't have a conversation.... Oh, no, even for Thanksgiving dinner we went out.... *(She laughs.)* Shayna calls me up and says, "Ma, we're going to a topless place for Thanksgiving dinner." I say, "A what place?" She says, "A topless place." So I think maybe this is a new name for some trendy kind of restaurant, but I don't say anything, because you know everything I say is wrong with those girls, and besides, I think maybe it'll be interesting. A good story to tell. "Yes, I'm eighty-two years old and my daughters took me to a topless bar for Thanksgiving dinner." As if Phyllis could top that! *(She laughs again.)* Hang on, I'm telling you.... So we get there, and right away I'm disappointed because everyone's got their clothes on. And on the menu it says "Tapas." T-A-P-A-S. I still don't know what it means. It's Mexican or something.... Yeah, it was okay. Salty, but good. Oh! and I had shrimp! Well, I only had one.... I was about to bite into the second one when my stupid daughter yells out, "Ma! What are you doing!? You can't eat that, it's not Kosher!" As if she's Kosher. As if she's been Kosher since the day she left this house. Who made her the Parve police?

(The whistle on the kettle starts to blow.)

MA: That's my tea. How was your Thanksgiving?

(MA gets up and walks toward the stove. BENNY enters from the back, ducks under the phone cord, but then is trapped by it as she walks past him. He waits for her to realize what she's done, but she doesn't appear to notice.)

MA: Uh huh... Oh, that was nice.... Uh huh... Really?

(MA puts some tea bags in a tea pot and then fills it with hot water. She waddles back to her chair, releasing BENNY from the coils of the phone cord without acknowledging him.)

(BENNY continues into the kitchen and sits. He does not turn on the T V. He merely stares at MA.)

MA: Oh, no. They got out Saturday morning before it got bad.... They never stay a whole weekend. Sharon says she needs Sunday to recover from the trip before she goes back to work. Recover from what, is what I want to know. She sleeps in a hotel, she eats at restaurants, she sits in my apartment and doesn't say anything. What's to recover from? And you know

Shayna, she won't visit when Sharon's not here....
*(She gets up again to pour her tea. She reaches into the
cupboard with a little groan.)* Oh no, Benny didn't go
to the topless place.... I don't know what he did.
Probably sat in the bathroom all evening, in his chair,
staring at the wall. You know....

*(MA takes down one cup, fills it with tea and sets it in front
of BENNY.)*

MA: Yeah. I'm going to worry all winter now, with him
going out for his walks. You remember last year with
his toes. It's amazing he walks at all now, but, you
know, nothing keeps him from his routine.... *(She gets
another tea cup pours some tea, spilling some. She looks for
the schmata on the hook.)* Dammit. Where's the? Where's
the schmata? Benny? Where's the—never mind, you're
useless. It's nothing. I just spilled some tea.

*(MA shuffles off to the back. BENNY is amused and
triumphant.)*

MA: I know.... I know....

*(Suddenly there's a loud thud, and the phone cord falls to the
floor. BENNY is startled but does not move.)*

MA: *(Off stage)* Oh! Oh! Benny! Help me. My hip! Oh,
I felt it pop! Benny! Will you do something! Ohhhhh.

*(After a moment BENNY jumps up. He goes into the back and
backs out holding the phone.)*

BENNY: Hello... Yeah... She fell.

MA: *(Off stage)* Benny, will you help me up!

BENNY: No, I can call.... Bye. *(He hangs up and dials 9-1-1.)*

MA: *(Off stage)* Ohhhh. How can you just leave me here?

BENNY: Yeah, hi. My mother fell on the floor. She wants
me to help her up, but I don't think I should.

(MA *groans in pain as the lights fade. the T Vs flicker in the darkness.* BENNY *paces, nervously, and then puts on his coat for comfort. He continues to pace. Then grabs the remote for* MA'*s T V and sits in her chair.*)

Scene 12

(BENNY *sits in* MA'*s chair watching T V. The volume is turned up loud. After a few moments the phone rings. He turns down the volume and looks at the phone. It rings a second time, then stops. He gets up and stands by the phone. After a moment the phone rings again. He picks up.*)

BENNY: Hi... Yeah, hi... I'm okay.... Yeah, it was good, thanks.... Oh. She is? ...Where am *I* going to sleep? ...Oh. Okay....No, I can do it.... Yeah.

(BENNY *hangs up the phone. He takes a long look at the arm chairs and the daybed and then begins to rearrange the furniture. He puts the daybed where* MA'*s chair was. He lays in the daybed, and finds that he cannot comfortably see the T V from there. He shifts the daybed. He arranges the armchairs in a suitable fashion, with one of them in the corner that the daybed occupied. He picks up his bedding from the floor and begins to lay it out on the daybed. He plumps the pillow and sets it carefully down. Then he moves it slightly. He stares at it all a moment. Then he picks up the pillow and sniffs it. He grabs the rest of the bedding and walks to the back rooms. Lights fade. the T Vs flicker in the darkness. In the half-light a paramedic helps* MA *back into the apartment and gets her into the daybed.* BENNY *comes in, not acknowledging anyone and pulls the walker out of the closet. He sets it up near* MA. *The paramedic exits.*)

Scene 13

(Lights up on MA *in the daybed, swaddled in blankets. A walker is to the left of the daybed.* BENNY *sits in an arm chair, opposite her. They both look over at the front door which is being pulled closed by the paramedic.)*

MA: *(Weary)* We'll be fine. Thank you.

(The door closes. BENNY *and* MA *lock eyes—* BENNY *tense and uncertain,* MA *tired and scared.)*

MA: Did they bring my pills?

BENNY: They're on the table. Do you want one?

MA: No, I...there's a schedule.... I don't know when—

BENNY: It's on this paper.

MA: Okay.

*(*BENNY *tries to hand* MA *the paper.)*

MA: No, you keep it. You'll have to tell me when.

(Long pause.)

MA: You were okay while I was gone?

BENNY: I was okay.

MA: You ate.

BENNY: I ate.

MA: Shayna said she stayed with you.

BENNY: Yeah. Some of the time.

MA: That was okay?

*(*BENNY *shrugs.)*

(After a moment, the phone rings. They both look at it, up on the wall. It rings a second time and then stops. BENNY *gets*

up and stands next to the phone. He and MA *continue to stare at one another.)*

MA: What are you doing?

(The phone rings again. BENNY *picks it up and holds the receiver to his ear, but says nothing for a moment.*

BENNY: ...I'm here.... Yeah...I got it.... Yeah... Thanks. I got it.... Yeah, she's here. She's okay. I thought you would come today. *(To* MA*)* You want to talk to Sharon?

*(*MA *wearily shakes her head "no".)*

BENNY: She doesn't want to talk to you.... I got it.... I know... I know! I KNOW!

*(*BENNY *hangs up the phone.* MA *and* BENNY *stare at one another for a long while. Suddenly he breaks their stare and goes to the kitchen. He pours some water in a glass and brings it to her.)*

MA: Your sisters are not relaxing people. I'm glad they went back home. Everyday in the hospital for two weeks. Sitting there. Fretting. I think they were hoping I'd die. Some days I was hoping I'd die, but something just makes you go on. Like it or not. I could hear them talking when they thought I was asleep. I heard Shayna say, "You know, these broken hips, they're usually the beginning of the end." And Sharon said, "I know." She didn't sound too unhappy, though.

*(*BENNY *sits in the arm chair and looks at* MA.*)*

MA: The beginning of the end. The beginning of the end has long since come and gone.

(Again they stare at one another.)

MA: Did you miss me?

*(*BENNY *stares at* MA *unresponsively.)*

MA: I have to go to the bathroom.

(BENNY *looks terrified at the prospect. He does not move.*)

MA: Could you pull the blankets? I can't move my legs.

(BENNY *carefully pulls the blankets out from around* MA's *legs. He then helps her set her feet on the floor. She grimaces in pain.*)

MA: Okay, okay. (*She lets out a long sigh.*)

MA: You remember how the guy showed us?

BENNY: (*Hopefully*) You want the walker?

MA: I'm not strong enough for the walker, yet.

(BENNY *steels himself, then bends down and puts his arm under* MA's *arm. He holds out his other hand for her to brace herself. She rocks herself in preparation as she counts.*)

MA: Okay. One, two, threeeowahhh! Ow. Okay.

BENNY: You're okay?

MA: Yeah.

BENNY: It hurts.

MA: Yes... Okay. I can walk now.

(*Very slowly* BENNY *walks* MA *off-stage.*)

MA: It's a good thing you're here, Benny? Otherwise I'd put Sharon and Shayna in the poor house. They wouldn't let me stay with them. They'd put me in a convalescent home. Or take me out back and shoot me like a horse, if they could get away with it.

(*Lights fade as they disappear into the back. The T Vs flicker in the darkness. In the half-darkness* BENNY *guides* MA *back to the daybed. He puts on his coat and leaves.*)

Scene 14

(Lights up as BENNY *enters from the stairway.* MA *is on the daybed watching T V.)*

MA: You're back. That was fast.

*(*BENNY *takes off his coat and hangs it up carefully.)*

MA: Didn't you buy anything?

BENNY: He wouldn't let me.

MA: Who wouldn't let you?

BENNY: Mister Schuller. He asked me to leave.

MA: Didn't you tell him I was sick?

*(*BENNY *paces frantically.)*

BENNY: No.

MA: I'm sure he's heard what's happened to me.

BENNY: He asked me to leave. In front of everybody.

MA: Oh, Benny. I'll call him. You've known Mister Schuller since you were five years old. He probably didn't recognize you.

BENNY: He knows who I am.

MA: Hand me the phone. I'll explain.

BENNY: No.

MA: I'll explain and you can go back.

BENNY: No...I can't do it.

MA: You can't do what? Go into the store?

BENNY: I can't...buy things.

MA: Of course you can. You buy cigarettes all the time.

BENNY: It's different. They know me. I don't have to
ask. I go in. I put my money on the counter. And they
know. Camels. No filter. They give me my change and
I leave. They don't look at me. They don't talk to me....
Everyone was staring at me.... He said I was too dirty.
That he'd have to throw out the tomatoes I touched.

MA: Oh Benny...

(BENNY *starts rocking slightly.*)

BENNY: I can't.... I can't.... It... It...hurts... To have them
all looking at me.

MA: *(Quiet, but firm)* Well, how are we going to eat?
I can't go to the store.

(BENNY *stares at his hands.*)

MA: I'll have to call your sisters. They'll figure
something out. Will you hand me the phone?

(BENNY *retrieves the phone for her.*)

MA: I want to know where this cordless phone is that
Shayna said she sent. Have you seen a box downstairs?

(Beat)

BENNY: There's a box.

MA: Is it for us?

BENNY: I don't know.

MA: Well, will you check, please? It's probably the
phone.

(BENNY *puts on his jacket, slowly buttoning every other
button.*)

MA: How long has it been there?

BENNY: I don't know. A few days.

MA: And you didn't think to see if it was for us?
Someone could have stolen it.

(BENNY *leaves as she talks.* MA *dials a number.*)

MA: Busy.

(MA *looks around a moment, then drops the receiver on the floor.* BENNY *comes back a few moments later with a smallish box. He hands it to her, then takes off his jacket and hangs it up carefully, meticulously.*)

MA: I can't open it, will you get me a knife?

(BENNY *hangs up the phone and gets* MA *a steak knife from the kitchen. She pokes at the box with it, but her hand is a little shaky.*)

MA: Maybe you should open it.

(MA *hands* BENNY *the box and the knife. He slices it open, pulls the lid up, hands it to her, and brings the knife back to the kitchen.*)

MA: Oh, look. There's a card. (*She pulls out the phone.*) Will you figure out how this works?

(BENNY *takes the phone over to the kitchen table. As* MA *talks he looks over the directions.*)

MA: "For our dearest mother on her birthday." My birthday was weeks ago. "How does it feel to be eighty-three?" Eighty-three! I'm not eighty-three.

BENNY: Yeah you are.

MA: No, I'm not, I'm only eighty. Eighty-one at the most.

BENNY: You're eighty-three.

MA: No... Really? ...This is a conspiracy. My children are trying to make me crazy. You're in cahoots with them. Eighty-three.

BENNY: I don't like this phone.

MA: I don't remember turning eighty-two.... I don't.... Did we do anything special when I turned eighty-two?

Did anyone visit me? ...I can't remember it at all.
(Pause) Did I hit my head when I fell? ...Benny?

BENNY: I don't know.

MA: Didn't you see?

BENNY: You were in the bathroom.

MA: Ever since I fell I've been....

(MA looks at BENNY. He is messing with the phone.)

MA: Do you think I was a good mother?

(BENNY looks at her a long moment, then goes back to poking at the phone.)

MA: How's the phone? Can you figure it out?

BENNY: It smells funny.

(Pause. MA looks at the card again.)

MA: Eighty-three. I should be dead by now.

(The lights fade. the T Vs flicker in the darkness.)

(In the half-light BENNY sets up the phone, and puts the old one away. MA pulls herself up with the walker and goes over to the waste basket to throw the card away. She goes back to the daybed and sits. BENNY pulls some things out of the refrigerator.)

(The faint sound of arguing can be heard, perhaps from downstairs, perhaps the T V, or perhaps from the depths of the past.)

MOTHER: *(V O)* You are not wearing that. You are not leaving this house.

DAUGHTER: *(V O)* I hate you!

MOTHER: *(V O)* Yeah, well, I hate you, too. Go change your clothes.

Scene 15

(Lights up on MA *sitting in her daybed, watching T V, flipping through channels.* BENNY *has just finished making sandwiches and is bringing one to* MA *as she talks on the phone.)*

MA: Who's your fourth now? ...Oh? How is she? You know, you're all welcome to come here to play. I can't move, but I could play cards. Thank you, Benny. Did you see that? He just brought my lunch. He's waiting on me hand and foot.... Shayna's got some sort of Internet service bringing us groceries. Otherwise I don't know what we'd do. Did you hear what happened with Benny over at Schuller's? It would be one thing if he'd never met Benny, but he's known him his whole life.... How can you say that, Lois? He's never attacked anyone. He's a lamb. He doesn't even talk to people.... Look, I've gotta eat my sandwich. Say hello to everyone for me.... You're not comfortable with it. Fine. Fine. Maybe someday I'll be well enough to come over to your place again.... Yes. Goodbye. *(Pause. She stares at the receiver.)* Benny, could you hang this up? I don't know which button. But leave it here. With me.

*(*BENNY *gets up, takes the phone, pushes a button, moves to return it to the wall, remembers, and with great effort sets it down next to* MA. *Meanwhile, she takes a bite of her sandwich.)*

MA: Euh! This tastes so funny. *(She peels up the bread.)* What is this? Is this tongue? It doesn't taste like tongue.

BENNY: It's ham.

MA: Ham!? These Internet people gave us ham?! Why didn't you tell me?

*(*BENNY *is eating his sandwich at the table.)*

BENNY: It's all they brought.

MA: You're going to eat it?

BENNY: It's all they brought. It's good.

(MA looks at her sandwich, then at BENNY. She takes a small bite and begins to giggle with her mouth full. He joins in.)

MA: A nice couple of Jews we are.

(They laugh for a moment, MA heartily, BENNY more subdued. After the laughter subsides, she sighs.)

MA: No one will come see me.

(MA sighs. BENNY looks on as the lights fade. the T Vs flicker in the darkness. She pulls herself up with the walker and goes in back. He begins to rearrange the furniture to its original set up.)

SPORTSCASTER: Stay tuned as March Madness continues....

WEATHERMAN: Folks, it's the longest day of the year, so enjoy, because they all get shorter from here on out.

COMMERCIAL: ...We've got costumes, candy, tricks and treats for all ages....

Scene 16

(BENNY sits at the kitchen table reading the newspaper. MA comes out from the back using her walker. She's in some kind of hurry. She wears a pretty dress that is not zipped in the back.)

MA: Benny, would you zip me please?

(BENNY stares at his mother, confused.)

MA: What're you looking at me for? I need to be zipped. I can't reach.

(BENNY gets up and gingerly zips up MA's dress.)

BENNY: Where are you going?

MA: Where am I going? Your sister's wedding. You've gotta help me find my purse. The green one. The one that goes with this dress.

(MA *maneuvers around* BENNY *and heads towards the pegs next to the door where his coat rests among other jackets.*)

MA: See if it's over there. On one of those hooks. Behind the coats.

(BENNY *places himself between* MA *and the door.*)

BENNY: Whose wedding?

MA: Shayna. Your sister. Don't you pay attention?

BENNY: I thought Shayna was married.

MA: You're not looking for my bag.

(*Pause.* BENNY *searches* MA*'s face.*)

BENNY: Who's she getting married to?

MA: She's getting married to Jonathan. Remember him? She brought him here and he brought us that nice pastry. She got divorced from that other loser. Kevin.

(*Pause*)

MA: What?

BENNY: Shayna didn't invite you to her wedding.

MA: Of course she... She didn't?

BENNY: Shayna married Jonathan in 1982 and she didn't invite you.

(MA *is taken aback. She's trying to remember, to get her bearings.*)

MA: What year is it now?

BENNY: Two thousand.

MA: Two thousand? (*She is completely baffled by this. She looks around the room, at herself, her walker.*)

MA: And she didn't invite me?

BENNY: No.

MA: Did she invite you?

BENNY: She didn't invite any of us.

(MA *begins to walk back to her room, sniffling as the lights fade. the T Vs flicker in the darkness. All the while a Christmas carol is being sung on T V:*)

T V: It's the most wonderful time of the year....

(*And then:*)

T V: If olde acquaintance be forgot and never brought to mind....

Scene 17

(MA *is sitting upright in her chair. She is waving her finger at someone who is not there.*)

MA: You never do anything around here! I cook, I clean, I wash your clothes. Stop crying! You're so selfish.

(BENNY *comes in the front door. He watches* MA, *neither surprised nor concerned at first. But maybe a little curious and irritated.*)

MA: Why do you waste your time with these things? No one cares if you can paint a picture. You don't get a husband by painting pictures. Men want a woman who can keep a good house. Give me those! I said give them to me! (*She reaches out towards the invisible person she's talking to.*)

BENNY: Don't hit her!

(MA *spins around.* BENNY *closes the door.*)

MA: Benny.

(MA *is disoriented for a moment.* BENNY *hangs up his coat in his usual meticulous way.*)

MA: You're back from your walk.

(BENNY *goes to the kitchen and starts making sandwiches.*)

MA: I was having the strangest...the strangest... Your sister. She was little. She was on the back steps. Not here. No. Where we used to live. When you were a baby. She was painting. She had made a...what do you call it? That painters lean their pictures on.

BENNY: An easel.

MA: Yes. An easel. I asked her to do the dishes, but she said, "No, I'm painting. Don't interrupt me."

(*Pause*)

MA: And I grabbed the paint sticks. The...the...the...

BENNY: Brushes.

MA: And I smeared them across the paper, mixing all the colors. I said, "That's what I think of your picture! Go wash the dishes!" And she was crying. Screaming....

BENNY: And you hit her.

(*Shocked,* MA *looks at* BENNY.)

MA: How do you know? How do you know about my dream?

BENNY: I was there. I remember it.

MA: In my dream?

(BENNY *looks at her for some glimmer of understanding, but does not find it. Lights fade. The T Vs flicker in the darkness.*)

Scene 18

(MA *sits in her chair talking on the cordless phone.*)

MA: I'm so glad to hear that. How's Kayla? What grade is she in now? She's doing well in school? ...That's good. Is she there? ...Oh, that's too bad. I haven't spoken to her in such a long time.... Oh, he's all right. I want you to talk to him though. He's been yelling at me.... I don't know. Because I can't remember things.... He doesn't like me asking him questions. He gets mad and he yells. I don't like to have people yell at me.... Is he? I don't remember. What time is it? Benny?! Benny!? ...Are you here?! *(Pause)* Sharon wants to speak to you. *(To Sharon)* I don't know if he's here.... Oh, you're right.... Yes, I see his coat.

(BENNY *has come out of the back silently and is standing right beside* MA.)

MA: Benny! Oh! Benny! Don't sneak up on me like that! Here.

(BENNY *holds the phone up to his ear.*)

BENNY: ...Yeah... Yeah? *(He glares at* MA *and turns away from her.)* ...Uh huh... I understand.... I'll try.... I know.... Yeah, okay, bye. *(He hangs the phone up and puts it in it's cradle on the other side of the room.)*

MA: I wasn't done talking.

BENNY: You were done.

MA: I didn't even get to ask about Kayla.

BENNY: You asked her eight times about Kayla. You ask everything eight times. A hundred times!

MA: You're yelling at me!

(BENNY *paces, trying to regain composure.*)

MA: Don't pace like that. You make me nervous.

BENNY: Do you want me to tell them about how you tried to go to synagogue at three in the morning? Do you want me to tell them those things? *(Muttering)* God you make me crazy!

MA: I don't remember that.

BENNY: You don't remember anything!

MA: Don't yell at me, Benny. Please don't yell at me.

(BENNY stalks off to the back. The bathroom door slams shut. MA is very upset, crying.)

MA: Oh. Oohhhh. Benny! I think I had an accident.... Benny?

(BENNY comes out, still mad but much calmer. He comes up and stands by MA.)

BENNY: I'm sorry.

(MA wipes her nose and eyes. BENNY holds out his hand, tenderly—for him.)

BENNY: Come on.

(MA looks at him. BENNY waits patiently. She places her hand in his. The lights fade. The T Vs flicker in the darkness. In the half-light he sets up his daybed for sleeping and lies down. She goes back to her room.)

Scene 19

(BENNY is asleep on the daybed. MA comes in with her walker. She goes over to the daybed and sits in the chair near his head. She turns the lamp on, awakening him.)

MA: Do you ever hear voices? *(No answer)* Sharon said that you told her once, a long time ago, that you heard voices. That a voice told you to go to the desert and that's why you went to California. *(Pause)* Do you still hear it? The voice?

(BENNY does not respond. MA turns back to the front.)

MA: Sometimes I think *I* hear voices.... I think I'm going crazy.

BENNY: You're just old.

(MA stands up and leans over BENNY.)

MA: Turn over.

(BENNY does not move.)

MA: Turn over.

(They look at one another for a long time. Then BENNY turns, and MA pulls up his shirt, searching at his back for something. Suddenly she freezes, then rubs a spot on his back, ever so gently. He stares out, expressionless.)

MA: You have a scar. *(She continues to feel it.)* It's so...

(MA pulls her hand away from BENNY and then takes her walker over to the arm chair and sits. She looks at him. He sits up. Pause)

MA: I was lying in bed and I just.... This vision of something flying across the room, hitting you in the back. I don't even remember what it was.

BENNY: It was a piece of an ash tray.

MA: How can you remember that? You were so little.

BENNY: You were throwing it at Shayna. You missed.

MA: ...No. No, I wasn't throwing it at....

BENNY: Because she burned the latkes.

(Pause. MA seems to remember.)

MA: Are there other scars?

(Pause)

BENNY: Probably. You'll have to ask them.

MA: Do you think that's why? ...Do you think that's why you're sick?

(Pause)

BENNY: No.

(MA holds her hand to her mouth, teary and afraid of her own thoughts.)

MA: I don't want to hear the voices, Benny. I don't want to remember.

(Lights fade. the T Vs flicker. MA goes to her chair. BENNY puts his bedding away.)

Scene 20

(MA sits in her armchair. BENNY is at the table.)

MA: Who was that woman who was here this morning?

BENNY: Marta.

MA: Who is she? Why is she coming here?

BENNY: To help.

MA: To help who?

(Pause)

BENNY: You.

MA: Me?

BENNY: Yes.

MA: How does she know about us?

BENNY: Sharon pays her to come.

MA: Sharon? ...She pays her to help me? ...Do, I know Sharon? *(Pause)* She was nice. This woman. What did you say her name was?

BENNY: Marta.

MA: Is she Jewish?

BENNY: I don't know.

MA: We should ask her.

BENNY: No, Ma.

MA: Why not? I want to know.

BENNY: It doesn't matter.

MA: Of course it matters.... I think she must be Jewish.
She's very nice. (*Pause*) I'm having a good day today,
don't you think? Could you take me for a walk later?
Just around the block? It looks nice outside.

BENNY: We went for a walk.

MA: Today?

BENNY: Yes. You don't remember.

MA: I know I don't remember, I know.... Sometimes
I think you lie to me. You tell me we went for a walk
because you know I don't remember, but we never had
a walk.... Tell me about it, Benny. Were there flowers?
Is it the time of year for flowers?

(*Lights fade. the T Vs flicker in the darkness. In the half-light*
BENNY *gets up and puts his coat on and exits. Then* MA *gets*
up, she straightens her wedding photo, and takes the photo of
her husband off the wall and carries it back over to her chair.
She wipes the dust from the photo and then embraces it.
Lights fade to black.)

Scene 21

(Lights up on MA *in her chair, her eyes closed. She holds the photo of her husband.* BENNY *comes in the front door and sees her asleep. He closes the door, not trying to be quiet. She does not stir. He hangs up his coat in his usual meticulous fashion. He goes to the kitchen and puts her pills in a paper cup. He pours her a glass of juice and brings everything over on a tray. He sets the tray down in front of her.)*

BENNY: Ma.

(Still, MA *does not stir. He pulls the photo from her grasp and her hands tumble lifelessly into her lap.)*

BENNY: Ma.

(No response. BENNY *shakes* MA*'s shoulder. She tilts to the side.)*

BENNY: Ma?

*(*BENNY *realizes* MA *is dead. He sits in the opposite arm chair and stares at her, holding the photo of his father much the way she had been holding it. Lights fade to black.)*

Scene 22

(Lights up on the apartment. It looks the same, except no one is in it. The phone rings twice and stops. It begins to ring again. After many rings, BENNY *comes in from the back room. He wears a suit which fits him well and is carrying a yarmulke. He is struggling with his tie which is hanging at odd lengths. He answers the phone.)*

BENNY: Hello? ...Yeah... No, I'm coming.... I'm ready.... I know.... I did.... I did.... I know! ...I DID! *(Pause)* I don't have to say anything, do I? ...Do I have to wear a tie? I can't tie it. I don't remember how.... Okay.... Sharon?

...Will I stay here? ...By myself? ...Who will pay the rent?
...Really? ...No, I want to.... No. I'll wait outside.

(BENNY *hangs up the phone. He is about to try again with
the tie, but he gives up and leaves it like it is. He is about to
put the yarmulke on, but then shoves it in his pocket instead.
He goes over and takes his shabby jacket off the peg. He starts
to button it over his suit, but then he realizes how that would
look. He takes it off and carefully hangs it back on the peg.
He stares at it a moment, then puts it back on, but does not
button it. He returns his parents' wedding photo to his
preferred skewed angle, then he goes out into the hall.
He looks over the empty apartment for a moment, then
pulls the door closed behind him. Lights fade.*)

END OF PLAY